To my Iwa bird:
Never doubt you came from greatness
and you are greatness.
Love Mama

World Map

This map uses the Peters Projection which accurately represents the land area of countries and continents.

Timeline

BCE: Before common era (before year zero)
CE: Common Era (year zero to present day)

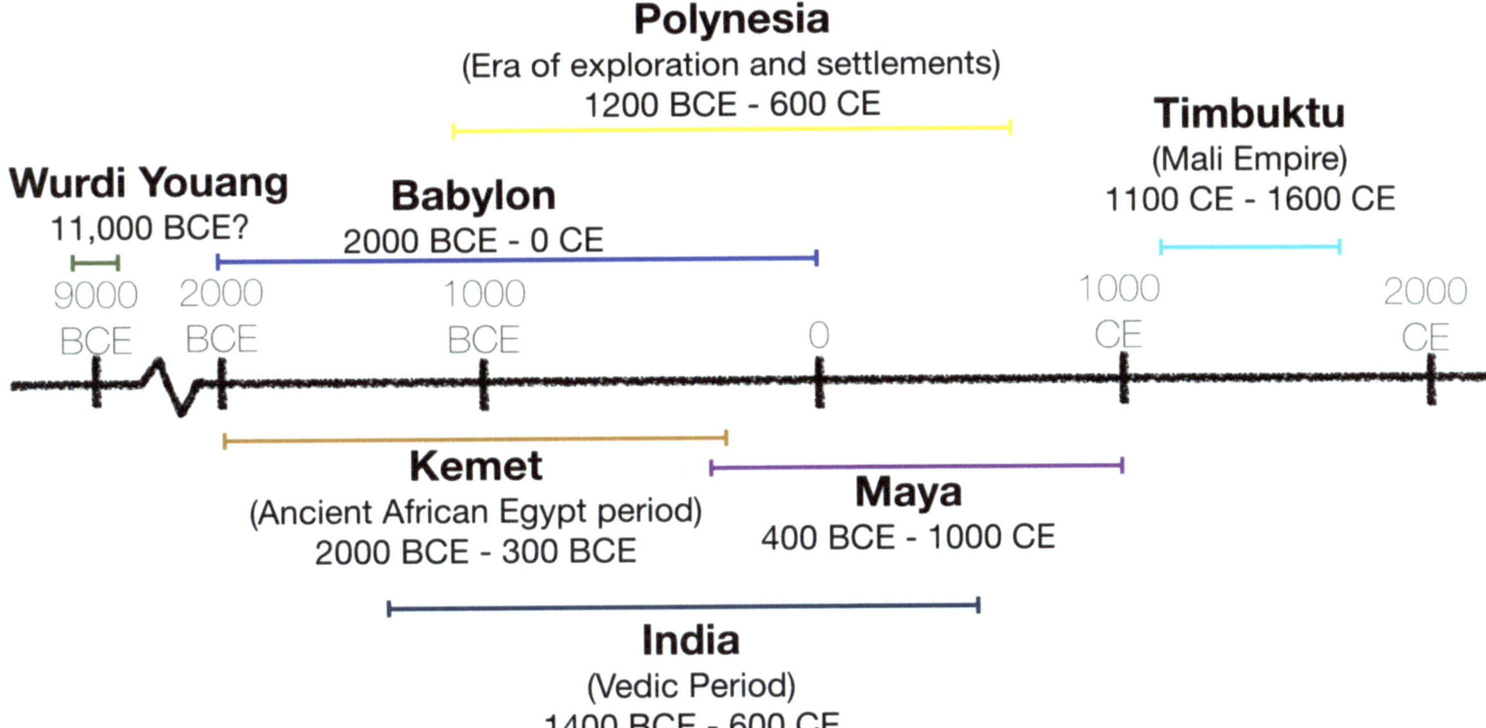

Pronunciation Guide:

some of these are estimations of pronunciation for languages that are no longer spoken

Sun

Gnomon: “no-men”
Wurdi Youang: “word-ee” “you-ang”

Kemet: “keh-met”

Kemite: “chem-aight”
Sopdet: “soap-debt”
Sahu: “sa-who”
Hatshepsut: “hat-shep-soot”
Senenmut: “se-nen-moot”
Akhet: “awk-het”
Peret: “Per-ret”
Shomu: “Show-moo”

Babylon

Nabû: “nah-boo”
Ištar: “ish-tar”
Śalbatānu: “Sal-baa-ta-new”
Cuneiform: “cue-ni-form”

Polynesia

Hokupa’a: “hoe-coo-pah-ah”
‘A’a: “ah-ah”
Newe: “Neh-veh”

Mayan

Nok ek: “knock-eck”
El caracol: “l-car-uh-coal”

India

Bhugol: “boo-gaul”
Aryabhatta: “are-ya-bot-ah”

Timbuktu

Al-katim “al-ka-teem”
Anhar: “an-har”

Did you know that our black and brown ancestors were the first scientists to be focused on the stars and the sky? What did they learn and see with just their eyes and observations?

Just as you look up in the night sky tonight, so did our ancestors that came before us. From all over the world these astronomers used their knowledge to learn about the stars and the planets, and honor them in their own way.

Before we read about our ancestors, let's talk about what they were looking at in the sky!

Planets

Our ancestors knew the planets were different from stars. With their eyes, they could see the 5 planets closest to Earth.

Today we call the 8 planets in our solar system Mercury, Venus, Earth, Mars, Jupiter, Saturn, Uranus, and Neptune.

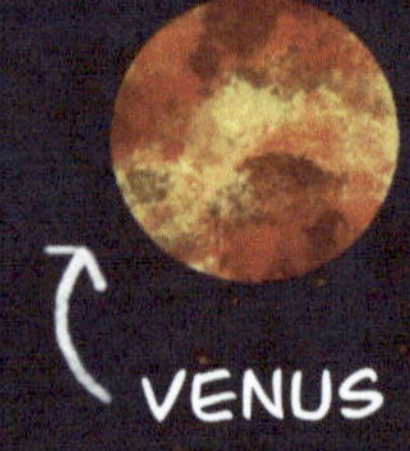

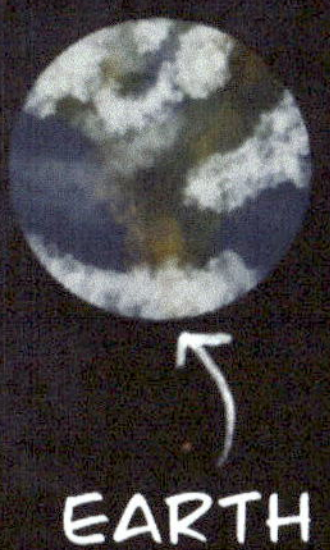

But our ancestors around the world gave them their original names. You will learn some of them as you read this book!

Stars

Stars are special.
They make their own light and shine on planets nearby. They are made of hot gases— hydrogen and helium.
Our very own Sun is a star!

Our ancestors relied on the stars to tell them when to plant food and the weather to come.

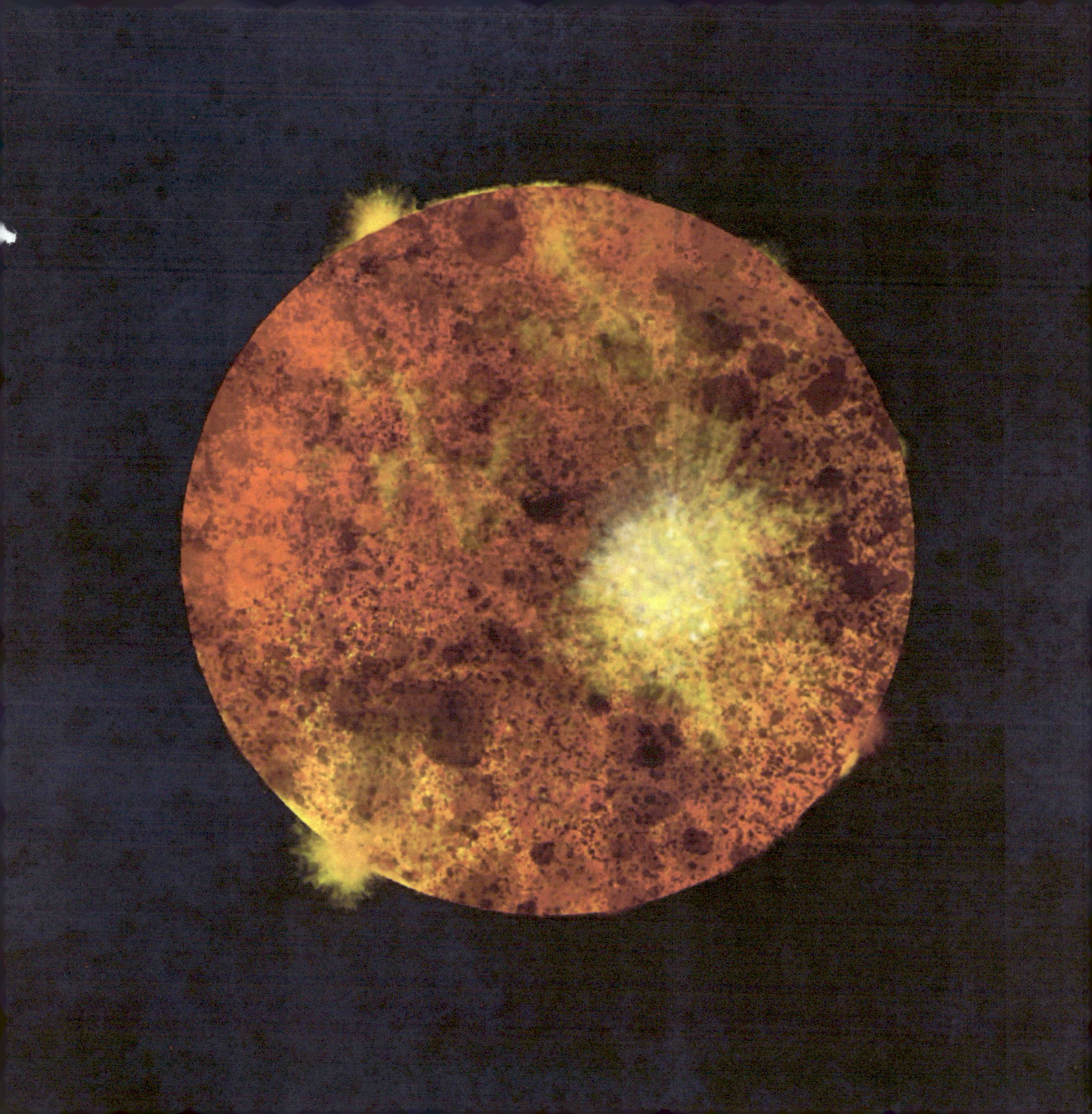

Some of the brightest stars in the sky had names given by our ancestors, like Sopdet or Hokupa'a.

Throughout this book you learn the names our ancestors used!

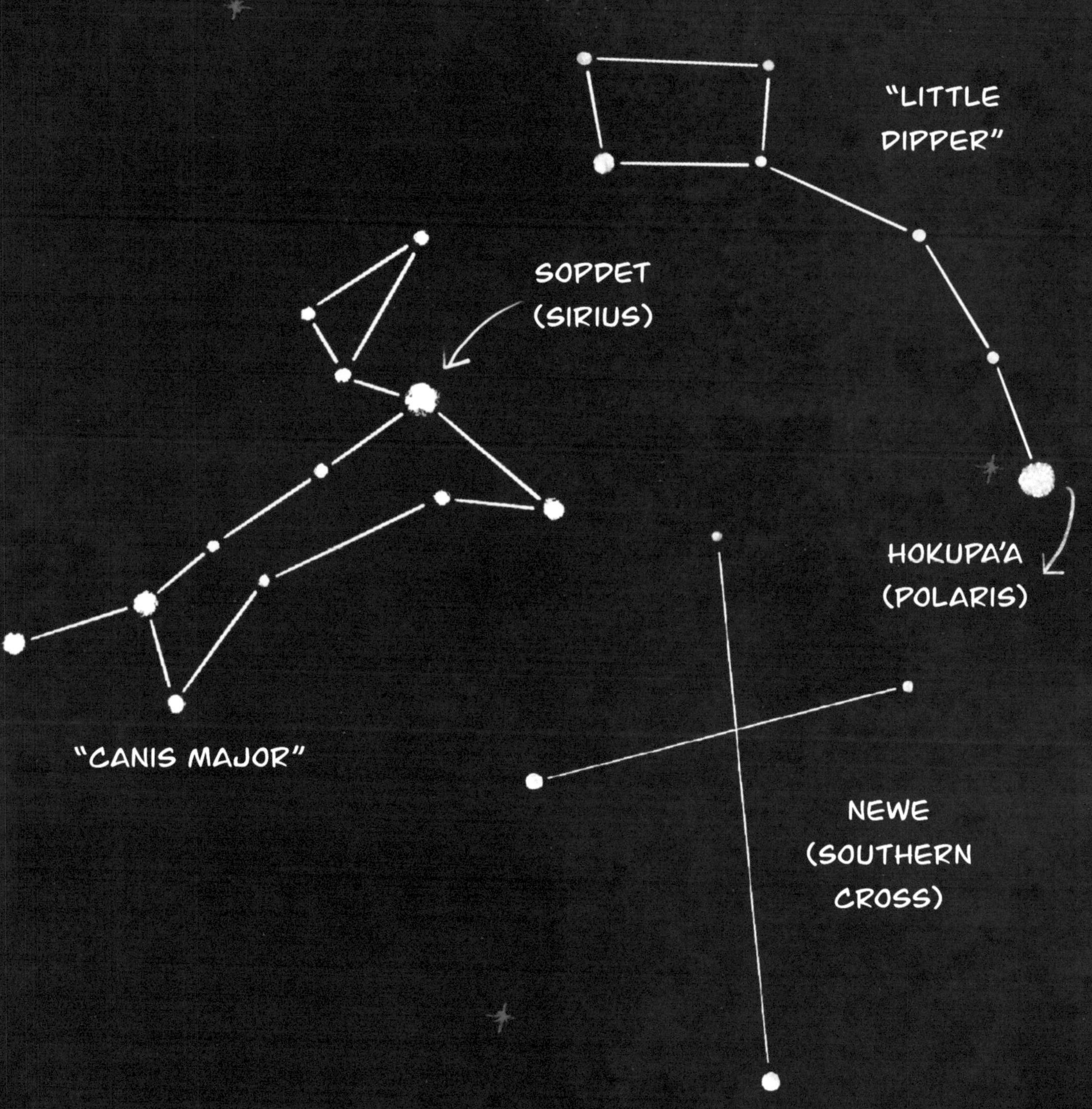
"LITTLE
DIPPER"
SOPDET
(SIRIUS)
HOKUPA'A
(POLARIS)
"CANIS MAJOR"
NEWE
(SOUTHERN
CROSS)

Sun

The Sun helped our ancestors to tell the time of day and even the season!

A gnomon stick tells the time of day, and the length of the shadow tells the season.

Our ancestors also created clocks and calendars from huge boulders! Two of the oldest that we know of are Nabta Playa in Kemet (Egypt) and Wurdi Youang in Australia.

NABTA PLAYA, EGYPT, AFRICA

EXAMPLE OF A GNOMON STICK

WURDI YOUANG, AUSTRALIA

Kemet

Hatshepsut was one of the first and most powerful female pharaoh. She built many temples and roads. One temple has unique drawings on the ceiling of star figures and a calendar!

It was the star Sopdet (Sirius) that told our ancestors about the seasons and when to plant food.

HATSHEPSUT TEMPLE,
KEMET, AFRICA

Polynesia

Our ancestors in the South Pacific used the stars to travel across entire seas and oceans!

They memorized star "families" and used their hands to know where they were. The brightest stars, Hokupa'a, 'A'a, and Newe told them where to go.

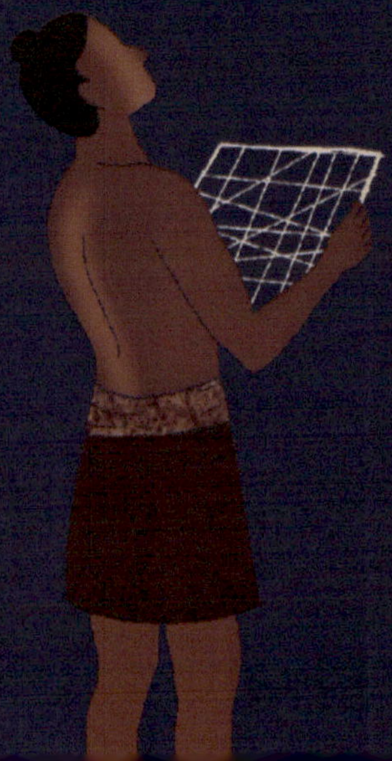

Mesoamerica

The Maya built an observatory to watch the brightest planet in the sky— Nok ek (Venus). The many tiny tiny windows let the Maya see Nok ek as it moved across the sky.

They even made a chart of where Nok ek would be in the sky into the future. This chart is still used by astronomers today!

THIS IS HOW THE MAYA WROTE THE WORD "NOK EK" (VENUS) →

EL CARACOL

CHICHEN ITZA, MEXICO

Babylon

To learn about the planets, the Babylonians made a new kind of math, Geometry! With this, they could tell which planets were closest to, and furthest from, Earth.

They wrote all of their knowledge in a language called Cuneiform, made up of triangles!

Nabû (Mercury)

Ištar (Venus)

Śalbatānu (Mars)

Šulpa'e (Jupiter)

Sagus (Saturn)

THE ISHTAR GATE,
BABYLON, MESOPOTAMIA

India

The Indian astronomer and mathematician Aryabhatta wrote about Bhugol (Earth) as a sphere and turning on it's own axis (center line). 1,500 years ago when Aryabhatta wrote, this was unheard of!

In fact, European astronomers didn't know this until 1000 years after Aryabhatta.

NALANDA UNIVERSITY,
INDIA

Timbuktu

In West Africa, the Mali Empire's main city of Timbuktu was known for its gold, salt, and books. It was the great Mansa Musa I who led the city to greatness.

He built Sankore University. Its library had one of the largest book collections in the world— up to 1 million books!

MANSA MUSA I

At the library, scholars wrote about all kinds of topics including astronomy!

One astronomer, Abulabas Al-Galawi from Timbuktu, wrote of 7 planets including Al-katim (Mercury), and Anhar (Mars). Al-Galawi's work, and other Islamic astronomers, would later help European astronomers.

SANKORE UNIVERSITY
TIMBUKTU, MALI

Look up to the stars, and look down to feel the earth beneath you. Today, we carry the strength, wisdom, and spirit of our ancestors.

They were leaders, scientists, engineers, and artists. They had big dreams and they achieved big things. What we know today about outer space began thousands of years ago with our ancestors.

Never forget that you came from this greatness. Celebrate who you are and the history you have come from!

Further Reading/Viewing:

Documentary: The Ancient Astronomers of Timbuktu (2009)

Learn about the Olmec, the precursor to the Mayans, thought to be African in descent: https://youtu.be/lSO-bFwMx2I

Take an immersive virtual tour of Ramesses VI's tomb (KV9): https://my.matterport.com/show/?m=NeiMEZa9d93&mls=1

Learn about Polynesian navigation on the Hokulea website: http://www.hokulea.com/education-at-sea/polynesian-navigation/

Turn the page to find coloring pages to enjoy!

Where are your ancestors from?

(mark it on this map)

WHAT DID YOUR ANCESTORS LOOK LIKE?

DRAW THEM HERE!

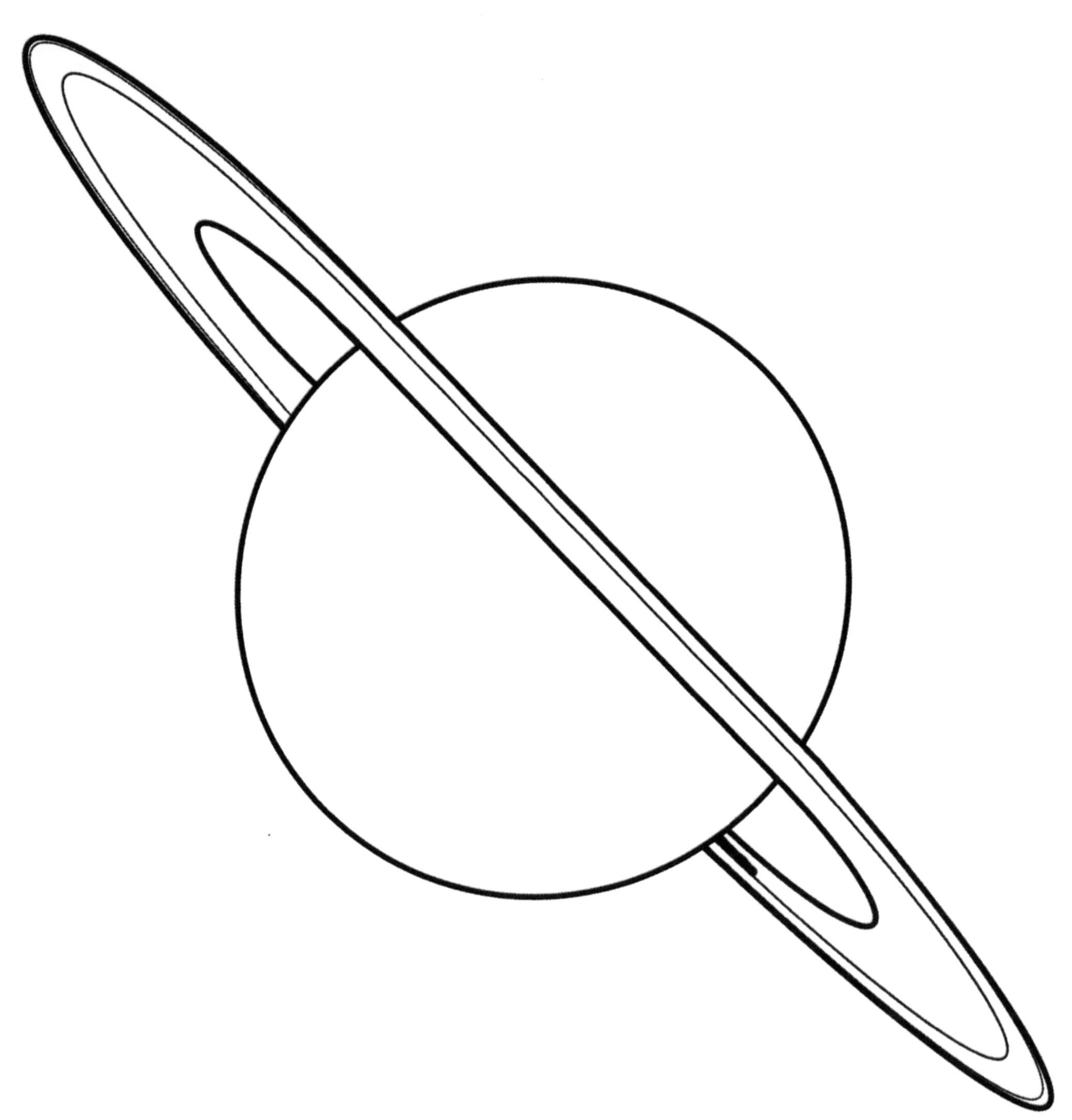

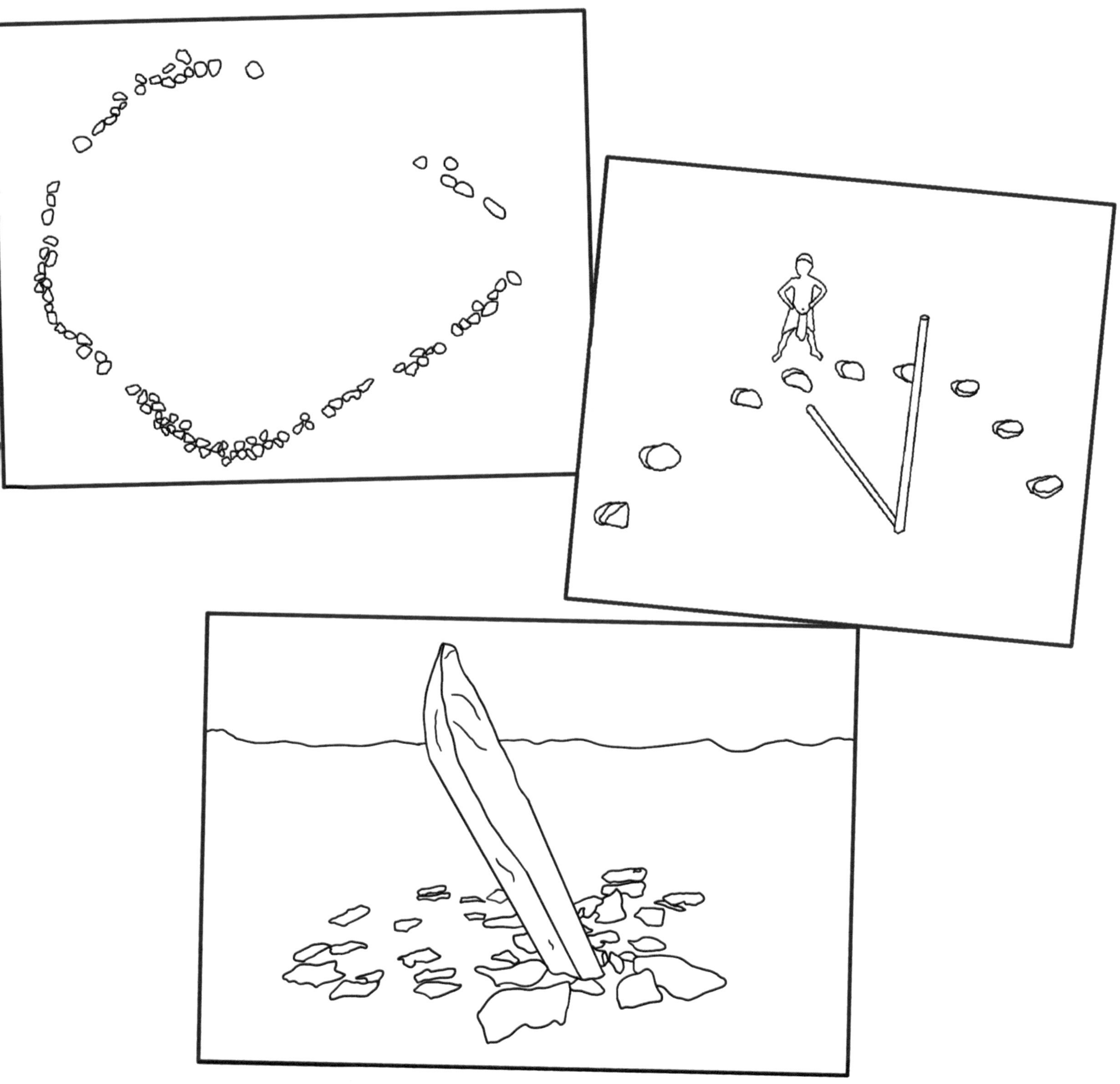

SANKORE UNIVERSITY,
TIMBUKTU, MALI

HATSHEPSUT TEMPLE,
KEMET, AFRICA

NALANDA UNIVERSITY,
INDIA

EL CARACOL
CHICHEN ITZA, MEXICO

www.ingramcontent.com/pod-product-compliance
Ingram Content Group UK Ltd.
Pitfield, Milton Keynes, MK11 3LW, UK
UKHW060112300726
14090UKWH00002B/151

* 9 7 9 8 7 8 1 0 0 9 8 5 5 *